The Hand That Guided Me

In the Midst of the Storm

Rebecca E. McMillan

authorHOUSE

AuthorHouse™
1663 Liberty Drive
Bloomington, IN 47403
www.authorhouse.com
Phone: 1 (800) 839-8640

Published by AuthorHouse 03/16/2016

ISBN: 978-1-5049-8557-4 (sc)
ISBN: 978-1-5049-8558-1 (e)

Contents

Contents

Introduction

I've had tribulations in my life, but I've overcome them by the mercy and grace of God and much prayer to my heavenly Father. God inspired me to share my life story because of all the changes that have taken place. I was laid off a job that I had held for sixteen years. During this time I felt the urge to begin writing my story. Early each morning after I woke up and took my shower, I would go into my spare room and start typing. Sometimes I would stop for lunch, and at other times I would continue until it was dark. There were times I didn't realize how late it was until I looked into the living room and saw the darkness. I would stop then to put a light on and have my dinner. Then I would go back to typing. I wanted to get in as much as I could every day.

I am writing my story to encourage, uplift, heal, and free those who have been bound by circumstances. I want to let them know they can achieve their goals once they put their minds to the task. I wrote my book to inspire those who think that they can't prevail, those who feel counted out; I want to let them know that, with God's help and belief in ourselves, all things are possible. You are one of a kind and wonderfully made in the image of God. You don't have to remain where you are. You can move on. Life is a journey, and we all are taking the trip.

There is a destiny, a plan for our lives, that God has for each of us. This course we must all take. I've been through the storm and the rain. With determination and perseverance, I have run the race and kept the faith, steadfast and immovable, always abiding in the work of the Lord. May you be blessed with an abundant life in God.

Chapter 1
Childhood Memories

I grew up in New Brunswick, New Jersey, in a three-room flat.
Our flat, situated in the middle of the row houses, was attached on
both sides. Just past our front door, there was a little hallway with a
small bathroom off to the right. Slightly further down, the hallway
opened out into the large kitchen, and at the far end of the kitchen,
a two-step staircase led down into our large bedroom.

We had two large rooms—a bedroom and a kitchen—and one
small bathroom. We had two double beds in our bedroom. Six of us
children slept in one of those beds, three at the head of the bed and
three at the foot. There were seven children in all; my baby sister
slept in the bed with my mom. Later my mother bought a twin bed
for my older brother and older sister. This left four of us in the big
bed. The new twin bed went in the kitchen by the wall, next to the
water heater. Our flat had only two small windows. The one in
the bedroom opened out into a dark alley, and the other window
was in the kitchen. Our bathroom was so small that it didn't have a
window. The kitchen was in the back of the house; when we looked
out the window, we were able to see into our neighbors' backyards.
We watched the neighbor kids as they played ball, rode their bikes,
and threw Frisbees for their barking dogs. After we finished our
chores, we ran out to join the rest of the gang.

Our bedroom also served as a family room. There we had a dresser
and a television that we watched together when we weren't outside
playing. At the foot of the two-step staircase, there was another
double bed across the hallway. To the left was another double-sized
bed by the wall. In the bedroom was a kerosene heater to keep
us warm. I remember going to the corner store to get a gallon of
kerosene to keep the heater going. At times when the lights weren't
on, we had a kerosene lantern to light the house.

When it snowed, my mother made a very special treat for us.
She wouldn't collect the first snow because of all the impurities,

1

but the second snow soon became delicious ice cream, and we always enjoyed that. During holidays my mom made mincemeat pie, and we enjoyed a big dinner. There weren't a lot of toys, but I remember getting a Tiny Tears doll and an Easy-Bake Oven for cakes. I made the best little cakes in that oven's small pan. I have another fond Christmas memory of trips to this big place for a Christmas party with lots of gifts.

When night came, I went to the projects to skate in the moonlight. I felt so free out in the air. Sometimes I went with our neighbors to skate in a big building on Commercial Avenue in New Brunswick. This facility was a recreation building for children. It had a basketball court, so I played basketball also. At times they hosted dances. Later this building was turned into a school.

In the city there was a recreation center for kids on New Street, not too far from where we lived. There we played checkers or Ping-Pong or just sat around talking to friends. In this recreation center, a dance was held every Friday night. The lights were dimmed a little, and the DJ would play oldies-but-goodies, such as "At the Hop." We walked to the dance; it was safe. In my neighborhood we always had a place to go. We had two movie theaters within walking distance. When summer came and school was out, we went to the Salvation Army for Bible study or arts and crafts with other children from the neighborhood. In our neighborhood, we could walk everywhere. No one bothered us because it was a safe place to grow up. Everybody knew each other, and we all got along.

My older sister loved beautiful clothes. I remember her gold prom dress hanging on the wall. She liked to wear her blue jeans to ride on motorcycles. My older sister was like a mother figure to me and my sisters. She was the one who'd shampoo and straighten our hair with a hot comb. I can remember ducking when she got to my head. On Saturday nights, she'd make curls the old-fashioned way. After she cut a brown paper bag into strips, she'd section my hair and roll each piece around a strip of the paper. Dixie Peach or Royal Crown grease worked well on our hair.

One day I went to the recreation center with those paper curlers in my hair. A girl asked if I was related to Buckwheat from *Little Rascals*. I didn't reply, but the experience was so painful that I never went outside in rollers again. To this day I won't be caught outside with rollers in my hair. It's important to me to have my attire and hair in order before I leave my house. Some events in childhood can affect a person's life into adulthood. From that day forward, I was always mindful about how I presented myself in public.

I learned other modes of mindfulness too. I learned to develop a life of prayer to take me through the day. My mom always encouraged me to attend Sunday school and church. I enjoyed learning about the Bible and reading God's Word; his hand was there during these early years. In the morning I prayed to God for a long life. I wanted to live long enough to see adulthood so I could have a husband before any children were born. My mother never married any of our fathers; I promised myself that I would not have children without a husband of my own to plan my family.

I also told God that I wanted a big bed. I didn't care if I had anyone with whom to share it. God's hand was there; my prayers were answered. My belief in God started as a child and continues today.

Here are some details of the life we led. When I was a little girl, I washed up at the bathroom sink and bathed in a big tin tub. One day the landlady had a shower installed in our flat. In the middle of the kitchen, we had a big red and white table with silver trim. It was surrounded by white chairs. My mom had a set of glasses with a matching pitcher that had fruit designs on the pitcher. The glasses were very colorful and pretty. She made Kool-Aid in that pitcher for us. My mother did her ironing for all her children on the table.

She brought our dresses in New Brunswick from one of the corner shops on George Street. My mom worked at a big department store on New Street in my neighborhood, which was a convenient place to shop. Everyone knew each other by name, and anything we needed was in our location. In our neighborhood, on one side of the street, we had a meat market with sawdust on the floor, a tire company, a furniture store, a Buster Brown shoe store, a food store, a few restaurants and bars, and the shoeshine man. In the summer a man with a wooden leg played the harmonica out front, and we could buy snowball treats in different flavors. Across the street were Abe's Bar, a car wash, and another bar, all right in front of the Raritan River.

My school was on Bayard Street, a couple of blocks from where I lived. I walked to and from school each day. On cold days, my mother made sure I wore a coat and snow leggings so I stayed warm. Sometimes I saw dogs. I thank God that they never jumped on me. During recess, our teacher gave each child peanut butter cookies and a small container of milk. School was fun, and I enjoyed it. Later I attended the Lord Sterling School on Nelson Street.

In the fourth grade, we had beans for dinner during the week. My mother came from a family of vegetarians, Seventh-day Adventists from Chattanooga, Tennessee. She would feed us lima beans, kidney beans, black-eyed peas, and pinto beans. You name the bean, and we ate it. None of my sisters were fat. For the most part, we were healthy. Only one or two of us ever had childhood diseases. Certainly we had a varied and tasty diet to support our health. Our Sunday meal consisted of fried chicken, collard greens, potato salad, and cornbread. Some Sundays we had fried chicken wings, french fries, and biscuits.

When Monday came, we went back to school. For weekday breakfasts we had tea and toast, a toasted and buttered roll, or rice. For lunch we had sandwiches or hamburgers. We also had canned spaghetti for lunch; I hated it then, and I hate it now. No matter what my mother made for us for lunch, we counted on those beans for dinner. They gave us plenty of vitamins.

When I was a little girl, my mom found out that I had a touch of polio. I had to wear braces to my knees with brown shoes. My mother took the braces off the shoes, but I still had to wear special shoes, which were the best. I had to wear special shoes; I couldn't wear just any shoe. I could run with the other kids in the back of the house.

I remember many activities for both fun and profit in our neighborhood. There was a flat roof in back of our apartment, and we would go onto the roof and jump down onto a mattress. That was fun. We made up our own games because we enjoyed being outdoors at every opportunity. I'd eat and run back outside to play with my friends. There were big boxes in the yard, discarded after my neighbors bought items for their apartments. My sister GG and I would play in these boxes with our friends next door. We made mud pies and cut leaves up for collard greens, and sometimes we made real lemonade to sell. There was fabric on the street from stores, so I would make pillows to sell. Then there was the construction workers' building. There were four project buildings on Burnett Street; these were eight stories high. My sister GG, the one next to me in age, watched with me as the builders ate lunch. Once they finished and went back to work, we would collect their soda bottles and return them to the store for the deposit. That was one way we made money.

In my neighborhood there was a soul food restaurant owned by Jim and his wife, who worked with him. They had a daughter and son. Everyone ate there. He served breakfast, lunch, and dinner. In the morning we could always get hot biscuits with sausage. The food was good. He was always busy with customers. God's hand was there because we always had food; if we did not, Jim and his wife would provide food for us. He also would let me earn extra money; whenever he needed something from the grocery store, he would call my mother and ask her if I could go to the store for him. Running errands for Jim was one of the ways I made money to put into my jar and save.

Since the early age of eight or nine, I was always doing something to make a dollar. I also started to work for two black barbers on Burnett Street, folding towels and sweeping the floors. I was always independent so that I could buy what I wanted. When houses were abandoned, my sister GG and I would go into them to lift up the linoleum on the floors and find change to buy candy.

There were lots of fields to play in, so we would run through the fields, playing with grasshoppers and putting june bugs on strings to fly around. When the lighting bugs came out at night, we would catch them and take their lights to put on our ears for earrings and on our fingers for rings; we made our fun. We played hide-and-seek.

Also there was another game—spin the bottle. After the bottle had spun, the person to whom it pointed was kissed; it had to be a boy. We jumped rope and played hopscotch, jacks with the ball, and marbles outside. We would take an eight-ounce can, turn it sideways, and stomp our feet on it to walk. It made a noise: *click, clack.* We would tie stings to sixteen-ounce cans and walk on them. This was how I learned to walk in high-heeled shoes. My brother and his friends used to make go-carts from wood and two tires to push down the street. We kept busy until night, and still there were things to do until we went inside for the night. I can never remember being bored as a child.

When it was time to go inside for lunch, I used to sit on the steps by the door because I didn't like the lunch meat my mother bought. It had some jelly stuff inside it, so I'd sit there, pick the jelly out, and throw it outside. Sometimes my mother made hamburgers. To stretch the meat, she would put oatmeal in them, which I hated. However, I ate it. During the day we would sometimes make ketchup sandwiches and mayonnaise sandwiches.

At my friend's house, from the backyard, we could smell his grandmother's cornbread. She would bake cornbread every day and put that big pan in the window to cool off for dinner while we kept playing.

There were also times when I'd stay inside and watch my mother iron our clothes on the kitchen table and cook. I always liked being in the house with her. In the morning my mother would toast bread on the stove. If she didn't have butter, she would use lard, and it tasted good, but nothing was like that Sunday meal I always anticipated. Another feature of home life was dishwashing. In my house everyone took turns washing dishes. No one got away with not washing the dishes after those good meals.

My older sister would eventually go to work for people in Highland Park. When I got a little older, I would go with her. For lunch at her workplace, they had the best lunch meat with hard rolls, so I always loved going with her. She made sure I had some money to buy ribbons for my hair and kept some for snacks.

My father lived with us for a while, driving an eighteen-wheeler for one of the biggest companies in North Brunswick. He started out washing the trucks and later went on to drive them. He drove from state to state and later started driving locally. He was an excellent driver. He drove a truck for forty-one years before retiring. Even after he was no longer living with us, he took care of all seven of us.

He'd come to take us to the shore to buy a bushel of crabs and bring them back home to cook. Then we would go off to the park. He would take us to Johnson Park or Commercial Avenue Park in New Brunswick. We would lie on the blankets and roll down the hill; that was fun.

I had my moments when I wanted to be alone. I would go to the college in New Brunswick on George Street to sit by the pond; I'd buy a sub, potato chips, and a soda. I would sit there and enjoy God's creation under the trees in the sun. There were times when I liked to be alone, but I had friends, and we'd play together sometimes.

With one friend I formed a singing group, Buster and the No Notes. Our designated place to practice was in the projects. We would book engagements, but every time we were supposed to sing, it would rain. We finally gave up on singing. This didn't stop the music in school. There was a piano in the school auditorium, upon which I would play boogie-woogie. In my free time, I helped out in the library, which I enjoyed. In the fourth grade, I enjoyed rain; we went outside to walk in the water as it ran down the street, and then the sun would come out as it rained.

That memory reminds me of an old saying, "If it rains while the sun shines, the devil is beating his wife." I heard a lot of old sayings when I was young. Another was, "If you see a black cat, go the other way." There were others: "Don't go under a ladder, because it's bad luck." "If you step on a crack, you break your mother's back." Over the years I learned to let superstitions go. Who has time to watch out for all that? God is greater than the power of superstition.

I remember that every morning, after waking up in this rooming house, all the children would draw near to a big heater to keep warm. I would never go near the heater. My mother and I would get dressed to catch the bus to New Brunswick. We would leave my sister behind, which she hated.

When my mother went shopping, she always brought us little red boots and shoes for school. I still like red, and my mother loved it. Most of our dresses had red in them. We would go shopping in New Brunswick and catch the bus back to Jamesburg later.

In the morning my hair was put into braids, two or three or sometimes five; there might be two in the back and one in the front. I didn't like this hairstyle. When I got older, I grew tired of braids. We moved to Somerville, and I started to do my own hair in a ponytail with a ribbon around it. My mom didn't like my hairstyle, but I said that I would wear no more braids.

At that point I started fifth grade. I walked to school, which wasn't too far from where I lived on Center Street by the tracks. We could hear the horn of the train every time it came by. After living there for a while, we got used to the noise. Moving there started a whole new life for us. This was the place where all my sisters were staying. It was a red brick building with four apartments, and we stayed upstairs on the second floor. Most of my sisters stayed together in one room, and one of my sisters shared a room with the girl I call my stepsister. When I arrived there, she was put into another room. I shared that room since I am the oldest. The girl I called my stepsister always slept with a chain on her door at night. That chain and her reason for using it gave rise to some drama.

One night, from my bed by the window, I heard someone coming up a ladder. It was God who woke me up to hear the person coming up the ladder. I jumped over my sister onto the floor, unlatched the chain on the door, and ran out of her room to call my uncle. He jumped up from his bed. He went to my stepsister's room. By the time my uncle got to the room, he was on his way back down the ladder, and he broke his leg. When my uncle looked down, he saw his stepson, who was an adult. There was never any mention of this episode. During those days adults were secretive about such events.

After that incident occurred, my grandmother begin to look for a big house to shelter my sisters and me. We were never in the house with her son. If no one was home when I got there, I could leave and go next door to be with the family I had grown up with in New Brunswick.

Chapter 2
God's Hand in My Life

I want to thank God for all he has done for me during my journey, which has included some medical crises. He spared my life despite the polio I suffered. My corrective shoes and braces helped a lot, and I played like the other kids. My walk is perfect. I have no limp, and I'm not bent over. I know God as a healer because God has healed me many times and seen that I got care when I needed it. Once I fell, hitting my head on a cinder block. My father was coming by; he picked me up in his arms and told me I had no business up there. There was a time I was riding my bike and my foot got stuck on a rusty nail. My foot bled heavily, and I thank God that it did. The doctor told my mom that if it hadn't bled like that, I could have caught lockjaw. Avoiding tentanus was a blessing. One day at the table, while eating watermelon, I tried to take the knife from my baby sister, and the inside part of my thumb got cut. My mother placed cobwebs on the cut and wrapped it up, and the bleeding stopped. While getting me ready for school one morning, my sister was combing my hair by the hot water tank; my dress caught on fire. I never felt the heat, but my older sister smelled something burning. She said, "It's you!" I must have been about nine and in fifth grade. The dress I was wearing was red plaid with a bow tie in the back. This was a color my Mom loved to dress us in. It had a crinoline in yellow, pink, and blue. It was a very pretty crinoline, and I liked the way it held my skirt out. However, it was very flammable. Afraid, I ran out the door, and the flames went up past my legs. While I was running outside, a friend of the family came across the field. Our friend saw me and put the fire out. Then I ran back into the house, and my older brother was waiting with a pot of cold water. He poured water over me to make sure all the fire was out. I ended up with blisters on my body. My older sister was still standing on the twin bed, which had an army blanket on it. No one had thought to throw the blanket over me. We had never been taught to stop, drop, and roll.

My whole dress was burned. I had third-degree burns on my backside, my waist, and on the right side of my body. My older sister took off my dress, which was sticking to my body, and put another dress on me. I was then taken to the hospital and washed with a saline solution, wrapped, and sent home.

I couldn't stay at my house on Burnett Street because we had to move. Everyone was leaving, so my sister arranged for me to stay with a friend in the projects. In this project apartment, I had my own room, and care was provided. A doctor made house calls. He burst the blisters, first spraying a cold spray on them and then popping them. I said, "That hurts!" because it was very painful. When I tried to get up, I realized I could not walk down the hall to the bathroom. Luckily for me, my father came by to check on me. Noticing my condition, he picked me up in his arms and took me to the nearest hospital.

The hospital personnel said that I should have been there a long time ago. Before beginning treatment, they had to scrape all the burned skin off my backside and right side. I had to have surgery— skin grafts. For the grafts to heal properly, I had to lie on my stomach for a while. At night they would bring me buttermilk, which I hated. They would leave it on my table, and by morning it would have spilled. Every morning they came to give me a shot. I would hide in the playroom, but the nurse always had a way of finding me. My stay in the hospital was pleasant because of the friends I met. I remember how my hospital friends and I would comb our hair with a wet comb in the morning. While at the hospital, I met a friend before she left the hospital; she gave me her flowers. Finally my mother came to take me home to Jamesburg. The hospital sent me home with a small can of yellow ointment that had to be applied to my right side and my backside.

Chapter 3
Abandoned

After a year went by, my grandmother brought a house in Plainfield, New Jersey, on Prescott Place. This was in 1960, after my mother left. It was God's hand that was with us; the people she left us with became our guardians. The state wanted to separate us, but my grandmother kept us together. At our new home, our front porch was nice; this was a lovely place to sit. Cactus plants grew on the side of the house.

There was a big backyard to play in. Trees grew in the backyard, and there were many bushes to trim. The house had plenty of rooms. It also had a full, finished basement with two big washtubs and an old-fashioned washing machine. My grandmother had chores for us almost every day. Some days a load of clothes had to be done before school and hung up outside on the line. When we returned home, the clothes had to be taken down, brought into the house, folded, and put into the proper drawers. The first floor had a kitchen with a back door; to the side was a parlor and the dining room, where Grandma entertained her guests and relatives during the holidays. We had to polish her silver and wash the good china before they came for dinner. We ate in the kitchen with all the other kids, and after dinner everything had to be cleaned up and put away. The next room was the living room, which had a big floor model television; every one would gather around to watch TV. On Friday night it was *Rawhide*, a popular Western series, and wrestling, which my grandmother liked. She would move back and forth as they wrestled. She served a special, traditional meal of fried fish and squash on Fridays.

There was a schedule on the refrigerator for us to follow every day. Some days my chore might be washing walls; the next day it might be cooking dinner for the family, which I hated. Because of my memories of burns, the last thing I wanted to do was to stand near a stove. But my grandmother insisted that I learn to cook, and I did. The first time I cooked, the roast beef wasn't done, and my grandmother said to put it back into the oven until it got done. I thought that would be my last time cooking, but she continued to give me a day to cook, just like everyone else.

We all had a day to iron clothes, and all the ironing had to be done that day because the next day was someone else's day to iron. The floors had to be mopped and the carpet vacuumed twice a week. The upstairs had four bedrooms. One bedroom was shared by my grandmother and the man I called *Uncle*, her husband. In the middle of the hall was my stepsister's bedroom. It was small but nice; it was a long room that ran off to the side by a window. The next room was for me and my sisters; this was a big room with a window leading to the rooftop. In this room were two double beds, a dresser, and a closet by the door. The next room was small; this was the room where one of Grandma's sons stayed. Next to his room was the bathroom, a place she was particular about. The bathroom had to be cleaned frequently. We had to clean the floor on our knees with a rag. When she wasn't there, I used the mop. Grandma would always say that she didn't want any water on her walls or inside the corners of the walls. I learned to clean well from Grandma's teaching.

Grandma was funny about me and my sisters; she didn't allow us to eat in other people's homes. She would give instructions before we arrived. She would say, "If they ask you if you are hungry, tell them *no*." She would feed us before we went to visit. When we arrived, the grown-ups would go into the dining room, leaving us in the living room to watch television. When offered food, we said what she had told us to say. My grandmother was very protective toward me and my sisters. She didn't trust the safety of food everywhere, and today I can respect her for that lesson.

Once we moved to Plainfield in 1960, I started sixth grade at Clinton Avenue School. I woke up for school every morning and walked back in the afternoon in the rain, snow, sleet, hail, or whatever the weather might be.

God was guiding me. I attended a holiness church on South Second Street. The pastor was part of the Division of Youth and Family

Services. We had to attend her church. Next door to her was another holiness church that everyone liked. During the week, this pastor would have services that offered the opportunity to kneel and call on Jesus. This was her prayer meeting time; afterward she served cookies and soda. I always enjoyed church, so I didn't mind going. The hand of God was always in my life. No one else in the house went to church. I loved wearing nice clothes to services and other venues. That's why I always kept a job after school. I could go downtown in Plainfield to buy my dress clothes for church and school and my play clothes for after school and weekends.

Chapter 4
School Days

In the following year, I was in seventh grade at Hubbard Junior High in Plainfield. I walked there with my friends every day. During the winters, on cold days, we would stop for hot chocolate and continue to school. I liked junior high school. We would change into our uniforms in the summer and go outside for gym. The activities were running and jumping with a long pole; the gym teacher would score students on the basis of how far they jumped in the sand. It was fun; I always enjoyed being outside. I wonder now what happened to that type of sport in school. My next class was home economics, which consisted of making an apron and learning how to cook. I loved this class because we could eat whatever the class cooked. I also had a class where each student had to act out an event without speaking, and the class had to guess what he or she was doing. The teacher seemed to pick me often, which I didn't like, so I changed classes to escape her class. I didn't feel like being in front of the class all the time. When I left, she said, "What's the matter? You can't handle it?" I gave no reply, just left and went into the art class. I didn't have to act out anything for anybody there. After growing up and experiencing life, though, I found that the class I had escaped gave me useful tools to help me in my life.

That class was a stepping stone to my future. It prepared students for the future by teaching them to stand up with confidence in front of people, but I didn't look at it that way until I had gained more experience. This class taught students how to act. We need every tool offered to us in school to achieve goals and to be successful. These tools are the stepping stones that take people to the next level.

There was another course I wanted to take, which was typing. I always liked precise work and felt that typing would be a good course, but I listened to some of my friends. My friends said it was hard, so I never pursued the course. Later my uncle told me

I should have taken the typing course because it would help me later. Time went on, and I begin to do different jobs. I realized that typing was a work activity I enjoyed and wished I had taken it earlier.

My school had many floors, and I made it to every class on time. We had a big cafeteria. I ate there when I did not walk to Park Avenue to get a hamburger with fries and a Coke. Sometimes I would walk to Park Avenue during my lunch time. I then walked back to school, I did a lot of walking. The school was new to me. One of the teachers had a student to help me, so we would go to a lot of the classes together. When the boys saw me, they would say, "Oh, you've got your shadow with you." My guide would reply, "Just shut up!"

She was very nice to me, but sometimes the boys weren't so nice. They would call me "liver lips" because my lips were full, but I paid them no mind. I always kept myself looking nice. Later, as I began to mature, those same guys ended up liking me. I paid them no attention. My grandmother was very strict, so I walked a chalk line. In her household, children did whatever she said. She put the fear of God, herself, and my uncle into us.

After school I would walk home with my friends. On the weekends I would babysit for friends because I wanted to buy silk stockings for school. My grandmother brought them for church only; she said, "If you want to wear them to school, you better buy them." When I left for school in the morning, I used to pack my stockings and garter belt in my bag with the books. I got away with it until she checked my dresser drawer and found them missing. That was when she told me that if I wanted to wear stockings to school, I better buy them. At that point I started working so that I could have stockings for school. I did not like to wear socks to school. When I saw what the other girls were wearing, I worked to buy some of the clothing I liked. Once I reached high school, in ninth grade, I became a mother's helper. After school I would walk a couple of blocks down the street to this lady's house to watch her kids until she came home.

Chapter 5
Working Days

There were chores for me to do at my employer's house before she arrived. I would vacuum the rug, feed the dog, iron some clothes, cook dinner for the family, make up the beds, and clean the bathrooms. When she arrived home, I could call for my cab to go home. I worked for her five days a week. On Sundays I always went to church on Monroe Avenue; God's hand was guiding me to attend when no one else in my house did. It wasn't too far from the house, so I could walk there. My grandmother believed in church on Sundays even though she never attended. If you didn't go to church, you didn't go anywhere. That was the rule in her house, and we followed it.

The holidays were my favorite times. I had to have a new outfit with shoes; my desire to wear nice clothes made me very independent. I didn't mind working and wasn't a lazy person. At Easter time I had shoes, gloves, and a hat, and everything had to match for me. Growing up with a guardian, I learned to take care of myself after my mother left us in 1959. There were many lessons to be learned, and I was willing to take the journey, whatever the cost or pain. Working in my grandmother's house, I learned to iron clothes very well for everyone in the household—my grandmother, my uncle, her husband, my baby sister, my niece Tinker Bell, whom I helped to raise, and myself.

These tasks made me good at what I did. My grandmother said, "You are the best ironer in the house." I began looking in the newspaper for jobs ironing to make money, and it paid off. I know it was God guiding me along the way. When a wife didn't have time to iron her husband's shirts, she would hire someone, and I would get the job. In the summer I would work in the factory to save for my new school clothes, winter coat, and boots.

On some weekends my grandmother took the family to South Jersey to visit her mother. They lived in the country on a corner lot with a peach tree and plum tree. We ate in the backyard. She had some pigs that we would feed from the dinner scraps. We enjoyed going there. We especially enjoyed her jelly cakes, which were good. The only thing I didn't like was the outhouse. To avoid using it, I would go down the street to my aunt's house.

Chapter 6
South Jersey

Life in Plainfield was becoming hectic with riots and police killings. My uncle realized that I needed a break from this atmosphere, so he took me to South Jersey for the summer. I didn't have to worry about hearing police sirens. It was very quiet, and there was a lot of room to play.

When we woke up during the summer, you could hear the crickets, and sometimes they would be jumping on the bed. My grandmother had another sister-in-law whom we visited in another town. She had a big house with an inside bathroom. I always enjoyed going to her house because she had a big garden with watermelons and lots of vegetables, such as collard greens, cabbage, string beans, tomatoes, and cucumbers. She would pickle the vegetables and put them in a barrow in the shed. My grandmother had a sister-in-law who lived in South Jersey as well. I stayed with them one summer for two months. My aunt cleaned houses in the daytime; in her spare time, she would go fishing, and whatever she caught was our dinner. She brought home small fish that were tasty and full of bones. Sometimes we had catfish, but I wouldn't eat them because of the way they looked. I ate so much fish that summer that I called my uncle and told him I was ready to come home, asking him to pick me up. My aunt in Plainfield still laughs about that time. She once wondered aloud who had told on her, and I admitted that I was the one who told him about eating fish every day, and we laughed.

The ride back from South Jersey was always as good as the trip there because my grandmother and uncle would stop for meals on the way back. Everyone in the car slept until the station wagon stopped. Then we would all wake up and jump out of the car for food. We enjoyed those times very much. The restaurant where we ate sold hot dogs, hamburgers, fries, ice cream, and more. After eating we would get back into the station wagon and continue home. It was nice to visit South Jersey, but it was always good to return home. As I got older, my grandmother said that I didn't have to go to her mother's house, so I would stay home, having fun with my friends on our block. When my birthday and my stepsister's birthday came, my grandmother would give us a party and invite some of our friends. On one birthday we wore green mohair dresses with stripes, high waists, and bow ties, and crowns on our heads.

Chapter 7
The Move to New Brunswick

Once I entered the eleventh grade, I decided to move back to New Brunswick with my father and his girlfriend. My sisters followed me later. This was where I finished my last two years of high school. I enjoyed meeting new friends. We lived in an apartment with three bedrooms. GG and I shared a room. Finally we both went to the same school. We walked to school or sometimes caught the bus. I had to take care of myself. Prom time was coming, so I had to purchase a dress and shoes and buy my pictures, yearbook, and ring. No one was going to do this for me; I had to do it myself. There was a map that I had to follow and a journey I had to take, and I took it with God guiding me all the way.

My brother and my other sister also lived in this apartment. I'll call her Dancer; she liked to dance and was good at it. This sister always made my stepmother laugh. She was always doing something and kept herself busy in my stepmother's belongings. She was nosy and could locate anything hidden. My stepmother worked at the college. Dancer would go with her sometimes to help, and they would bring food home. We would be waiting for them. On the weekends the college had dances, and my stepmother invited me and my sisters to come. She had cold cuts, coleslaw, and baked beans, all of which she made really well. I always enjoyed her baked beans, and I still cook them the same way.

When I left Plainfield to move in with my father, I needed a name for my stepmother, so we called her Ma Dear. She was heavy and about five feet and eight inches tall; she was a woman who didn't play. My father knew she didn't play, so he was careful about how he dealt with her. My sisters and I were also careful. When she got on my brother about something, he just laughed. That house was a fun house; we had good times. After school I would throw my books down to watch *The Edge of Night,* a soap opera. It was very interesting and so deep that it was discontinued.

After dinner we would sit outside on the porch, laughing and talking with each other. so My sisters called me Mom Mack because I was the oldest. They always wanted to know if I was home.

When I got to New Brunswick, I was wearing a size seven. I never thought about my weight until I became a size fourteen from eating dinner food for breakfast. My stepmother cooked so well that we would eat what she had cooked for dinner that morning. She would come home from work and look in the pantry for the food, and it would be gone.

She was a good cook from down South; her dishes were short ribs, potato salad, collard greens, chicken and dumpings, barbecued ribs, biscuits, and candied yams—all kinds of soul food. We feasted but did not watch our weight, which wasn't good. I later had to deal with the weight because I had to buy another dress size. My stepmother was in the Elks, and they had parties that we would attend, bringing our own food. One year there was a contest for the title of Ms. Elks. The contestant who brought in the most money won the contest. I won.

In my school there was a sewing class that I liked very much, and I was good at making my outfits. For one contest I made a very pretty, short-sleeved gold satin dress. My picture was in the newspaper of my home town.

That weekend there was a parade for the Elks in Asbury Park, New Jersey. As the winner of the contest, I was in the parade. My outfit was a long pink and white gown with white gloves. I sat at the back of a convertible and waved to the people as we rode along. It was exciting to me. My stepmother seemed to have an interest in me. Whenever something was going on, she tried to make me a part of it. She got me into a church fashion show once. The fashion show was held upstairs in the church, and one of my dresses was brown with a big pink bow and polka dots.

This was the church I had enjoyed. and the Spirit was always high there. I knew a lot of people there. At that church I was later baptized. God guided me to join the church. It's good to have a church home and to enjoy fellowship with the people.

During this time, I was still living with my father, going to school every day, and working after school at a college on the hot-dish line and in the teachers' cafeteria, where I did the cooking. The cafeteria served hot sandwiches, other hot foods, and salads. I did inventory for the job and worked in the dish room. I always kept my finances together so I could take care of myself. I would do my homework in school during one of my free classes. When I returned home from work, I could take a bath and get ready for school the next day.

In my life, education was always important despite the cost and the journey. God continued to have his hand in my life and guided me throughout my school days. I had made up my mind to go all the way until graduation. My school was big. I enjoyed my classes, especially chemistry and the sewing class. I made beautiful dresses, slacks, and a skirt in the sewing class. I seemed to have a special ability in chemistry. It came easily to me, and my grades were good. With a push from a concerned adult, I could have done something in that field.

I have a passion to help others. Getting burned in my early years gave me a desire to be a nurse. This passion changed soon when I started dealing with fashion in modeling school. I graduated in 1967 from high school in New Brunswick. I continued to reside in that town and work at the college. Once I received my diploma, my supervisor offered me a job as a supervisor. Because I thought it would involve dealing with too many personalities, I refused the position.

Chapter 8
Life without My Father

After my graduation from high school, my stepmother left my
father, and he became very bitter. One day when I returned home,
I looked in the window and didn't see my picture, which had
been hanging on the wall in the hall. I went to find out what had
happened to the picture and saw my picture in the garbage can. I
picked the picture up and brought it back into the house. I put it
back on the wall. My sisters were the first ones to notice the picture
missing. It was normally visible through the window from outside.
They asked, "What happened to Ma Mack's picture?" *Ma Mack*
was my nickname that my sisters gave me because they all looked
up to me.

When I approached my father concerning my picture, he never said
a word. My father was so bad that he would take the fuse out of the
box when he knew it was time for us to go out. We started getting
ready in the daytime rather than the evening. Then, one day when
we came home, he looked at us and said, "All of you, get out."

We left, though we didn't have a place to go. I packed a bag and
left for my sister's house. This arrangement didn't work out well,
and the next day I had to make a phone call. I asked Ma Dear if
I could stay with her temporarily until I got my own place. The
hand of God was with me because Ma Dear had extra rooms, so
that dilemma worked out perfectly for me. In the meantime, I
was looking for an apartment. I met someone who worked with
the young people and asked him if he knew where I could get an
apartment. He told me about an apartment that was available, and I
knew this blessing was from God's hand.

Ma Dear, who had come through for me in my trouble, was a
strong woman with standards that we dared not cross. If she
asked us to do something, we did it without asking any questions.
She was a cook at Rutgers University and a truant officer for
New Brunswick High School. She was a foster parent to various

children. She took foster children in and gave them love and attention. She enjoyed life to the fullest extent. I remain grateful for her stalwart support when I found myself homeless and at many other times.

I went to check the place out, spoke to the landlord, and got the apartment. It didn't take me long to move in. The apartment was of a nice size with two bedrooms, a living room, a kitchen, and a bathroom. I had no problem furnishing the apartment. There was a salesman who went from door to door, and I bought my refrigerator, the self-defrosting kind, from him. I also got curtains. My sister had a friend who cosigned for me to get furniture for three rooms. My new sofa was a green and gold sectional. I already had my bedroom set, so I just had to buy two twin beds. My sister, whom I called the "knee baby," stayed with me sometimes. I continued to work for the college in New Brunswick. I walked to work every morning at 10:30 AM and worked until 8:00 PM.

When I got off, I walked back home when I didn't get a ride with a friend. I had all intentions of going to school to learn a trade, but it was important to put a roof over my head first. While I was working at the college, one of the ladies from my church invited me to speak at her school in Newark. I accepted the offer while wondering what my topic would be. My first impulse was to speak from the heart. I would share some of my experiences and how it was important to prioritize tasks. I was nervous, but once I started to speak, I felt a lot better. The teacher told me later that what I shared was exactly what the students needed to hear. This praise made me feel good.

Chapter 9
My Soul Mate

My first priority was to put a roof over my head, and everything else came after that roof. I intended to go to a trade school, but I had to prioritize my plans. It was important to keep working so I could take care of myself; no one else would. I was on my own, and later something special happened to me. God's hand, once again, moved in my life.

While working at the college, I met the man who was to become my husband. One day, while walking past the bakery shop, I saw a man standing in the doorway. He took a second look at me. I found out later that his name was Theo. I was friends with his aunt and talked to her every day. Theo saw me that day and told his aunt that he wanted to take me out on a date. My reply to her was, "Tell him to ask me!" and he did. He was a man with a beautiful smile and white teeth, one who never stopped smiling whenever I saw him. If he didn't speak, he would always smile; at times he was a man of very few words.

We dated for about two years while still working at the college. On the weekends we would go to the beach, attend the movies, or visit his relatives. I was able to meet every one except his mother and some of his aunts, uncles, and cousins who still lived in Florida and Alabama. During the third year, he told his aunt, to whom he was close, that he wanted to marry me.

"Tell him to ask me," I told her. He did, and later he took me down to the jewelry store to pick out a diamond ring. We got engaged, and the photographer came to my apartment to take my picture for the newspaper. He came with a big, bright light to shine on me, making everything exciting. Our engagement lasted five months, and then we married. My stepmother, Ma Dear, helped me plan my wedding. It was held at one of the restaurants in New Brunswick. It was a very nice place that was popular in the neighborhood. She also made sure we were able to do a waltz, which was our first dance.

I picked out my gown from one of the popular stores in Highland Park. My dress had a full skirt that was like Cinderella's, with lace and a long veil on its headpiece. My maid of honor was my best friend, someone I grew up with and hung out with after school. I chose my flower girls—my baby sister, a younger sister, and my stepsister, whom my stepmother had raised. The colors I had chosen were green for my maid of honor and yellow and white for the flower girls. My husband-to-be wore a black tuxedo with a white shirt. The date of our wedding was July 26, 1969. We practiced several times at the church for the wedding on Friday, and that Saturday we were married by my minister.

I had asked my father to give me away, and he said, "Yes." When it was time for me to get married, he had changed his mind. He said, "Get your brother to give you away." This hurt me so badly. I thought about my uncle, who had taken my sisters and me in. I asked him, and he consented. During this time of transition, I continued to work at the college. I didn't have to worry about eating because I got my meals at my workplace. Many other practical tasks required my attention.

To set up my apartment, I had bought sheet sets, blankets, pots, pans, silverware, and dishes. With those purchases, I had a good start for my new place. I ordered many items from a catalog. My sister's friend cosigned for me to get three rooms of furniture from one of the stores on Route 18 in East Brunswick. There was a salesman who came around from house to house, and from him I bought a self-defrosting refrigerator. On Georges Road I bought a Zenith television. My apartment was furnished by me alone. When I married, we didn't have to buy anything. My future husband had a car. Our start together was a good one. We had everything needed to complete our life together. The church was beautiful and joyful with all my guests and friends. We had a photographer, though others also took pictures. My stepmother was my coordinator. She took care of all plans, even the last five hundred dollars owed for the hall.

After the wedding, everyone went straight to the reception hall. We had already taken pictures in front of my apartment before we left. Once the bridal party arrived for the reception, Ma Dear announced each person who walked into the hall, making an arch for me and my husband to walk through. We had our first dance; when the dance was over, we took our seats to get ready for a toast by my maid of honor and the best man, who was my new husband's best friend. The table was set nicely, and I was happy, feeling wonderful about marrying someone who loved me for who I was and no other reason. Later the meal was served, and everyone ate. When we completed our meal, we walked around to each table and greeted the guests. I felt it was important to spend some personal time, touch our guests, and give them an opportunity to touch us.

Creating that moment was a pleasure for me. After we greeted the guests, it was time to open our gifts. We had many gifts to open. We couldn't open them all. I opened some, but the rest were taken home and placed on the single beds in the spare room. The next day we traveled to Florida and met the rest of my husband's family. I met my mother-in-law, with whom I had been speaking on the phone and exchanging letters. She sounded very sweet when we talked.

My wedding trip was my first time traveling in the South, and it was a long, hot ride. While there I met everyone, and they treated me kindly. My mother-in-law is a good cook. She made good biscuits in the morning and made sure the bed had nice sheets on it for me. It was extra special; everyone called me "Rabbit's wife" because *Rabbit* was my husband's nickname.

While visiting in Florida, I got sick from being in a different climate. I felt so weak that my husband took me to a doctor. He said I needed to eat more fruit, which helped me to feel better. We stayed in Florida about a week while visiting all his people. At the end of the week, I was ready to leave and come back home. It was good to get back home to New Jersey and see what everyone had given us for our wedding.

Chapter 10
Married Life

We stayed in our apartment on Seamen Street for another seven months. Then we moved into a house. We rented the first floor on Power Street. Before we moved, my brother-in-law and my husband taught me how to drive. My husband took me out to practice driving on a stick shift. The majority of my driving lessons were given by my brother-in-law, who taught me how to drive well—especially how to back up. I learned to drive in almost no time. I got my license.

We only had one car, and for that reason, I had to take my husband to work and then drive to work. My husband had a second job so at night, so I would pick him up at night. I continued to work at the college. Later my husband left the bakery shop at the college for a better job where he earned more money. He wanted me to leave also. Eventually I found another job at a computer company. Its facility had air conditioning and was very clean. It was a desk job. I worked with some nice women.

One day while returning home from work, I stopped by the car dealership. There I spotted a 1971 T-37, burnt orange with a beige top and very pretty. When I got home and told my husband about the car, he went to the dealer with me to see the car. I liked it, and he gave me the down payment. He said that all I had to do was to make the car payment every month. The payment wasn't too high. I was happy, and I was also tired of driving the stick shift—especially in the summer, holding that clutch on a hill. It had been fun at first to drive the stick shift, but the automatic was a lot less work for me.

This purchase was timely because I started with a new company then too. My new workplace had a big cafeteria and plenty of work space. When I started, I had two weeks of training in core repair before joining the other workers on the floor. After doing the core repair, my next assignment was to do memory boards for computers. I liked this work very much; I had my own workstation. While working at the computer company, I went to data-processing school every Thursday night. The location was in the truck stop building. They offered typing and keypunching, a six-month program. While I was going to school, my job had a layoff.

In 1970 I searched for a job in keypunching. I got a job at a cookie plant in Sayreville. Working in the office, I earned eighty dollars a week by keypunching and verifying the work. I also sorted the keypunch cards in the sorter and signed checks for the company. It was also my job to take the report upstairs in the financial department and business office. We had other companies coming in to visit the plant, and I was chosen as a tour guide for them.

Whenever new cookies were made, we got to sample them. There were always cookies in our office. Breakfast in the morning began to put weight on me, so I joined a gym to stay in shape. I went three times a week to exercise and use the sauna and steam room. While working in the office for the cookie factory, I found out that I could make much more money keypunching. I started searching in other companies for keypunching jobs. I found another job where I earned more money. It was a freeze at the time but I still made more money. After the freeze was over, they gave me a ten-dollar raise, which was excellent. I worked in a big office with a lot of girls, all doing keypunching. Everyone was friendly, and my supervisor appreciated the work I did.

In 1972, while working at my new job, I became pregnant. After my colleagues had given me a shower, I took a leave. The people I had worked with were great. Our relationships continued even after I left the job. We would meet on the weekends for dinner. There was a special friend who invited me to her house, and I met her family.

My husband was working for a chemical company. Before the baby was born, he went to work for a garbage company. He drove a big Mack® Truck. He picked up compaction units at different companies and dumped them. He started early in the morning and returned home around three o'clock in the afternoon. He did

four or five of these units a day. He worked two jobs, but before it
was time for me to deliver my baby, he quit the second job to be
with me. We had planned to start our family after being married
for about two years. That interval gave us time to spend with each
other and get to know one another a little better before having
a baby. He was very good to me, and sometimes he would cook
dinner while I watched TV. Sometimes I would cook, and he would
wash the dishes. We worked hand in hand, helping one another.
Our marriage wasn't a one-way street; when the baby arrived, we
were settled, and our household ran smoothly.

When it was time to go to the hospital, my husband took me there,
and my oldest sister went with me. I'd had a good pregnancy and
had never been sick. I had done a lot of driving, including trips to
Atlantic City for the weekend and to Asbury Park for fun.

I went to the hospital at midnight. I stayed in labor all night and
almost all day. The next day, finally, at five o'clock, my sister said,
"She can't deliver that baby naturally. She needs a C-section." My
doctor checked me and realized I couldn't deliver on my own. He
took me down to the operating room to deliver my baby. They
asked if I would like be awake, and I said no. I wanted to be out,
and I got my request. When I woke up, they told me I'd had a boy,
and I went back to sleep. I think having a C-section is hard because
later it's difficult to get up and hold your baby. Finally I was able to
hold him so that I could feed him on my own. When the time came
to go home, my husband took me. It was hard for me to do stairs.
I had to stay upstairs for a while. Thank God the bathroom was
upstairs.

My neighbor and her daughters were really nice. They made sure
my breakfast was sent over in the morning, and my husband fed
me at night. He was a good man! The minute he came into the
house, the first thing he did was to run up the stairs to shower.
He then came to get the baby; he would always give me a break
when he returned home from work. We would have dinner and
later watch TV as he played with the baby. Living in a duplex
was exciting and not expensive in the seventies. I liked having an
upstairs and downstairs with a washer, a dryer, a backyard, and a

driveway where we could park our cars. Because my kitchen was small, we made a dining room section off the living room. Every day the neighborhood kids would come to visit me and my son. They would take him outside for a walk; they all liked to hold him because he was warm. When they were a little cold, they would snuggle him close. Once they were warm, they would return him to me, and I would laugh. My neighbor's children were so good to me. When I was able to go out of the house after my six-week checkup, they would babysit for me.

My husband was a good driver. He taught me to back into the driveway. I backed the car up so when it was time to go home after work, I wouldn't have back up and pull up. It was hard trying to get out in such a big company because they had a lot of people working there. This technique came in handy and made it easy to get around. Today I still back into a spot; very seldom do I pull into a parking space. My driveway had a fence on both sides, but I had no problem parking between the two fences because he had taught me well. On the weekends while I was asleep, my husband went to get the cars washed. He would return later and polish both of them. He kept my car clean, and I didn't have to do anything to it. I would get up, take a bath, and prepare breakfast for us.

Later in the day, we would take a ride to the park or to the shore. Sometimes we went to visit a relative. We loved the movies and cookouts. On Sundays we attended church in New Brunswick, where I was baptized and became a member. My husband later joined the church also. This was a day of worship and giving thanks to God. My dinner was done early that morning, a tradition from my grandmother, who had raised me when my mother left. It was good to have a husband; someone who loved me so much and only had eyes for me. It's good to know when someone loves you, and I knew, in my heart, that he loved me and my son. He was a provider, a friend, a protector, a lover, a father, and a husband, one who didn't mind taking on responsibility. My husband was a man who always had a smile for me, showing his big, pretty, white teeth. He was a quiet man of very few words, but he would always give others a smile, and people liked him a lot.

When I wanted to shop, he didn't mind going with me. We also did the laundry together. Folding up the sheets, he would take one end of the sheet, I would take the other end, and we would meet in the middle. In our marriage, we tried to do many activities together, which paid off in the long run. Many of my friends, who had broken with their significant others, asked us how we stayed together. We told them that we enjoyed a lot of togetherness and that it was important to spend time with one's husband or wife. The purpose of being married is to have someone special for companionship and to build a family. God meant for us to have a helpmate and to be fruitful and multiply in the land. I enjoyed every day that I was married to my husband.

We marry to have a partner. Why go in separate directions when you have a mate? God didn't make us to be alone. God meant for us to have helpmates. There were very special activities that we did together. When there was a disagreement, we made up before going to sleep at night. We never went to bed mad at each other; there was no baggage to carry throughout the day. Anger causes separation; it pulls couples further and further apart. It's important to spend time with your mate before children come into the picture. Children can have your undivided attention when you have built a relationship before they come. We also had our social life. At our house we had parties. We invited other couples over to entertain them. We played music in the living room, danced, and served food. Sometimes we were invited to other couples' houses for a party or picnic.

There were nice couples around my husband and me. We enjoyed others' company, including that of the person who did my hair. I would invite him and his wife to my house, but we had one fault in his view. He liked to cut my hair after it had grown. My husband told me to tell him not to cut my hair because my hair was long, and he liked it that way. He was particular when it came to me; there was no playing around or offending me. My husband was very protective of me.

My husband loved me and took very good care of me. I couldn't have married a better person. I know it was the hand of God that brought this man into my life. We were married three years and eight months. Our wedding day was July 26, 1969. We waited for a couple of years before having a family. We wanted to get to know one another and enjoy each other's company before planning a baby. This was a wise decision; the two of us agreed with God on the matter. A couple needs a chance to know each other before bringing a little one into the picture. Children take a lot of your time, and it's good to share the responsibility with your mate. It makes life a lot easier and sweeter.

After giving birth to my son, I went back to work. I resumed work when he was five months old. It was in the winter, and bringing him out in the cold early mornings wasn't good. He caught a bad cold, so I had to quit and keep him inside. Once he got better, I went back to work for a tire company in New Brunswick. I started out keypunching. Later, when the supervisor saw my qualifications, I moved on to data entry. I always enjoyed my son during this time; he was a joy to me and my husband. We loved watching him grow up. We took pictures at every opportunity. We wanted to take pictures because he did a lot of new things and was growing quickly. We didn't want to miss any of his major milestones.

Chapter 11
My Life Changes Drastically

In 1973 I was working for a large company, and the pay was pretty good. We were getting ready to look for a house one Saturday in April, and something came up. We had to reschedule for the next Saturday. During the next week, I received a phone call, while working, from my son's godmother. She told me to come home right away and to take my time. When I arrived home, my son's godmother told me something had happened to my husband, and she had to drive me to the hospital in Plainfield. She drove me to Plainfield. While traveling, she told me my husband had an accident on Route 22 in Plainfield. Inside the hospital she walked me inside and to the elevators. We went up to the intensive care unit to see my husband, who was unconscious.

When I saw him, I just cried and stood there, looking at him in that bed and not saying anything, just hoping and praying he would wake up. After visiting my husband, I went to the waiting room to speak with his bosses. They informed me about the accident and tried to tell me what happened to my husband. His bosses tried to put my mind at ease, saying they would do everything possible to make sure he would receive care. This was the saddest day in my life. He was the world to me, and seeing him in that condition shut me down. I couldn't eat or sleep. During this tragedy, however, God's hand kept me sane and helped me not to be bitter about the situation.

I called all of his family and mine to the hospital after the doctor said my husband's situation didn't look good. He had lacerations of the brain. If he lived, he might survive in a vegetative state. We all took turns sitting with him. I stayed there day and night and only went home to shower, change clothes, and check on my son. My son's godmother and her kids were so good to us. They stepped right in and helped me take care of my son until I was able to return home. It was hard to eat anything. I lost my appetite. My in-laws would bring food to the hospital, and I tried to eat a little to keep going.

The accident had happened on a Thursday morning. My husband was driving back up Route 22 West in Plainfield, New Jersey, by the Blue Star Shopping Center. This was early on April 26, 1973. Rain poured down. He had just dropped off a unit for one of the companies, and his truck went out of control. It went onto the curb by a telephone pole and back out into the highway. The telephone pole cracked in half and fell on top of his truck, knocking him out of the truck head first. He went into the highway in the rain. The impact caused brain damage. All this happened on a Thursday morning, and I stayed with him in the hospital all day and night. On Saturday night we were sitting in the waiting room. We heard a code nine and wondered who it was. Later the nurse came to tell us that the code had been for Theo. They resuscitated him after a heart attack. About nine o'clock, they called everyone into his room to tell us he was gone. I stood there by his bed, screaming and crying and not believing he was gone. Knowing I wouldn't see him again, I had a lonely ride home.

Once home, I went next door to get my baby. I thanked God that I had Theo's son to remember Theo by. The night was long, and I couldn't sleep. All I could think about was my husband's accident. Knowing I wouldn't see him again devastated me. The next day people came from near and far to visit me. They brought plenty of food, which I hardly ate. I didn't feel like eating and started to lose a lot of weight. One day my oldest sister came by and asked, "Where is Rebecca?" Someone said, "She's over there." My sister said I had lost so much weight that she didn't know who I was.

Going through all this grief was hard for me. I wondered what I was going to do now that my husband was dead. How was I going to make it? He was my protector and provider, one who had taken very good care of me and my son. My confidence was in Theo, and when he died, I felt it was all gone. It was the hand of God that brought me through this great tragedy.

The days went by, and people continued coming to keep me company, especially the kids in the neighborhood. They were a big help and came to play with my son, who was six months old at the time of my husband's death. My son was the glue that held me together because I knew I had to keep it together to take care of him. I felt that no one would raise him the way I would. There were days when I could just sit and look at him. The kids from the neighborhood would say, "You love him," and I would reply, "Yes, I do."

I was always concerned about how I would take care of my son and myself. I told those who asked how we would make out that I didn't know, but I believed we would be fine and that God would provide for us. A professional person told me I could get Social Security for my son and myself. My husband's job gave us a check every month, which kept us going. My husband had everything in his name, so the insurance covered my cars once he died. He was a wise young man who thought ahead and also trusted in God, the creator of all things.

Losing my husband gave me a stronger prayer life and increased my faith in God. My family tragedy gave me a deeper walk with God. This tragedy brought a greater stability and helped me to hold on and to believe in God's ability to make a change in my life. The Bible says that "weeping may endure for a night, but joy comes in the morning." A prayer life dried up my tears and took away my loneliness. I had to ask God to take these feelings from me, and he did. My house was furnished with blue and white. Blue and white are peaceful colors that calmed others who came into my house. After moving to Somerset, New Jersey, a whole new world opened up to me. I gained new connections and helped other people in need.

Chapter 12
Reflections of Life

Losing one's true love is not an easy experience. There was so
much pain and sorrow that I cried almost every day. My friend who
had been my maid of honor came by to visit and console me. At
times, while talking to her, I would drift off and then come back.
She later said, "I was praying for you to get better every day," and I
did get better after a while. Prayer and the hand of God on my life
brought me through this tragic time. I took about a year to accept
the fact that I was all alone.

On the day of the funeral, my whole family and my in-laws were
there. My son's godmother took care of my son for me on the day
of the funeral. The funeral home took care of all my business,
which was a big help. They drove me to the funeral home and
helped pick the grave site. During this time of loss, I didn't do very
much driving. There were too many memories. I had to wait a
while before getting behind the wheel. Once the funeral was over, I
began to settle down a little. Then I was able to collect my thoughts
and resume driving. We had two cars. Before his accident, my
husband had just brought a brand-new 1973 Pontiac Grand Prix.
My husband had taught me how to drive the new car because it was
a little bigger than my T-37. I thank God for what he taught me. I
was able to pull the car up into the driveway. I had become more
familiar with my smaller car.

As time went on, I started to drive the T-37 sometimes and the
Pontiac Grand Prix other days. Ultimately I sold my car and kept
his. There were still some lonely days. I would stand in my door
and look outside, wondering what was going on in someone else's
house because mine was so lonely. I couldn't sleep at night and felt
that a change of environment would help. I started traveling around
to different towns. I was looking for a new place where I might rest
and gain some peace of mind. The hand of God was with me. One
day in 1974, I came across a place in Somerset, New Jersey. That

same night I packed my stuff. My neighbor's kids helped me move, leaving only a green rug. I went back the next day to take it up.

The next day it snowed very hard. I had to go to the public services department to start my electric and gas service. I left to take care of business. This was the best move for me—to get away from the house where Theo and I had lived together and to make a fresh start. I went to sleep at night and rested better. My neighbors were very nice and helpful. My son got bigger. His first Christmas was exciting; I tried to buy one of every toy in the store. His godmother said, "Rebecca, there is next year," and I just laughed. It was important for him to have a good Christmas, and shopping always made me feel good. When he reached school age, he started school.

I worked for a big computer school, a job that I liked. My coworkers liked me very much. The manager of this school called me one day after the main person had left the job. I had temped for the company for several months and learned their system very well, so I was the perfect person for the job. He made me an offer, which I accepted. I would work for the company for several years, running the whole keypunch department. Later I had a different boss. I helped this second boss a lot and showed him how to make up the program cards to do a particular job. I could bring my son to work with me when he wasn't in school, and it gave him the opportunity to learn computers early. I temped for some of the biggest corporations in the 1980s. My work paid my bills and kept a roof over our heads; my earnings gave us the opportunity to travel and take a few flights.

I think we need to take time to smell the roses and have some fun. When we schedule in some downtime, we are refreshed and ready to go when the new week begins. As a well-trained employee working for corporate offices, I was rewarded with my own space and an hour for lunch. My lunch time was spent at the park. I sat by the water there and ate my lunch. My lunch hour refreshed me for the afternoon. At the company I met a lot of nice people and became friends with some of them, but as time went on, I could see some changes happening and jobs being cut. Thank God it was time for me to move on.

My next assignment involved entering medical records into the computers for each individual school. While working there I met a nurse who invited me to eat lunch with her every day, and while eating she told me about her sister. This sister was the CEO of a company that was just starting to use computers. Perhaps, she thought, I might be interested in a position there. I'll call my nurse friend Mrs. Helpful—she said they had been doing data entry manually and were ready to upgrade. I called the company and made an appointment for an interview. The day of my interview, I wore a navy blue suit, white blouse, and navy blue shoes and carried a navy blue bag. That same day I got the job. I asked for a letter to confirm my position and was hired on September 30, 1991.

My office was on the second floor, though sometimes I worked on the first floor, answering the telephones for the company. There was much work ahead. The forms had to be put together in a format, organized by department, numbered on each page, and color coded. I wasn't a data-processing person at the time, so I needed help to make up the forms. I asked one of the managers to get her sister to organize the forms for us. When the forms returned to the office, my job really started. I had to learn a whole new system and what went into each location. This learning took some time, but I was determined to master the material.

Work in a medical field with nurses was a whole new world for me. I had to learn medical terminology, of which I had no knowledge. This made my situation hard Finally one of the managers gave me a seven-page manual of medical terminology that I studied to learn the nurses' language. I had to know how to code diagnoses and medicines, also what box to put each group of resources in to complete a whole form. It was a challenge, but I was determined to learn and to make the CEO very proud of me. I had at least twenty-five years of experience in data entry but was underestimated. This was a whole new world for me, but my entry into it was made easy by my friends praying for me. Meanwhile I prayed for the sick in the hospitals, doing my pastoral care. I saw this activity as an assignment from God because I had experienced a calling from God in 1978.

Chapter 13
My Son

When I stopped working, I stayed at home for a while and later took my son to a babysitter. From this sitter, he learned karate, and he was good at it. A friend continued to teach him karate as he got older. My son learned to walk at nine months. At that time we went to Disney World with my brother-in-law to visit "It's a Small World." I loved the Magic Kingdom, which was a place of healing for me. In this place one could escape all the cares of the world.

While my son was in school, I worked part-time jobs so that I could be home to meet him after school. Most of my jobs came through temporary agencies. I gained a wide range of excellent companies to work for and much experience in keypunching and data entry. The work had to be entered into the computer after I created the program card. Then I had to verify the work that was keyed into the computer. As time went on and technology changed, the work was keyed directly into the database; I had to be accurate with my assignments. This was the type of work I enjoyed.

When I came back from vacation, I went to work for a temporary agency. I worked there for about seven years because it gave me the flexibility I needed. I was able to be home when my son got out of school. My work for different companies helped to increase my skills, giving me more options. This gave me the opportunity to put my son in preschool at two and a half.

I had never told him how his father died. When he got older and started school, he began to ask about his father. I told my son that Theo had died in a truck accident when he was six months old. He was so young when his dad died that he had no memories of Theo. He took it pretty well, hugged me, and then asked to see a picture of his father. He took the picture and kept looking at his father. He put it on the dresser to remember his father always.

The days went by, and he continued to ask about his father. I kept subject of my husband's death open for him to ask questions whenever he felt ready. There were days we would talk about my husband's death and cry; he started to say he wanted to see his father. Theo wasn't coming back, so every day was a healing process for the two of us, and by the help of God, we made it through the days. When he got older, I took him to my uncle's house to play with his kids. This gave him an outing for some weekends, and he learned to ride his bike and play kickball, basketball, and baseball. He played football and was very good. He seemed to have a gift for that game. My son went to Catholic school for one year and then to public school in Somerset, New Jersey. He went to first grade and continued in public school. Once he attended public school, I would take him to school in the morning, and he walked back with my neighbors whenever I didn't pick him up. He learned the importance of reading at an early age from a book contest. The child who read the most books got a prize or certificate. He did well.

Rashan also joined the Boy Scouts, an activity he loved. He loved being outside. As a child he often stayed outside—flying a kite, building a fort, riding a dirt bike, and playing football. My son always had broad shoulders and was built like a football player. When he was old enough to play football, I signed him up for Pop Warner football, He performed well and enjoyed the games. I also introduced him to instruments and found he liked the organ, so he played it for a while.

I often took him to the mall, parks, movies, and skating rink. Some of my friends and I took our children to the skating rink for classes. We all got on the skates which fun was giving me my own personal skates. This is one sport that makes me feel free and special. When I watch skaters on TV, I wish sometimes that I was a skater. Skating is hard work, however, and you have to be very dedicated to it. I love to see when the people throw the flowers out and the stuff animal that's so special.

Being outdoors gives me a good feeling. The park is one of my favorite places to walk or just sit and watch the ducks fly and then dive into the water. One of the prettiest times is when the sun sets and the sky turns different colors, pink and blue clouds with the sun setting behind them.

My son always enjoyed riding the roller coasters and fast rides, which I didn't like. After riding them for a while, I felt sick. All these activities I've mentioned are some that I like to do on my weekends and sometimes after work. I call this fun *a refreshing moment*. We also enjoyed going into the city and shopping for clothes. One time we went to the circus, which I loved. I think I enjoyed it more than my son did. Later, after our refreshing moments, we would have dinner before we left for the ride home on the bus. We would walk down the streets and just enjoy the scenery whenever I wasn't driving to the shore, a place my son loved.

The boardwalk is one of my favorite places; the fun of trying to win a prize excites me because I love stuffed animals. I have them all over my room. Being by the ocean is relaxing and refreshing for the mind and body. I love eating some good food like a hot dog, shrimp and fries, or corn on the cob. And let's not forget a funnel cake and ice cream cone on the way home.

While Rashan was going to school, I always tried to make sure he was in school before going to work. That certainty was important to me. Safety was always my main priority when it came to my child.

My son has never liked waiting for anyone to put a toy together. He would do it himself. I would ask later, "How did you do that?" and Rashan would say, "I figured it out." When he got older, he could read the instructions and put anything together. He still has this skill. I brought an Atari for Christmas, and he hooked up all the wires by himself with no help, just through determination. He is electronically inclined and loves working with his hands.

We did many activities together; when you saw me, you saw him. It was important to attend church every Sunday; people would see him in church with me until he turned sixteen. My son was a homebody until he turned sixteen. He seemed to change at that age and stayed outside a lot. We would ordinarily have dinner together and eat a full-course meal, but then he started wanting pizza or fast food. When I shopped, I always brought special treats for him, such as big bottles of Hi-C® and snack packs. He couldn't drink regular milk, so I had to give him soy milk. I started feeding him grits and eggs, foods that would keep him healthy. I also made fried chicken and collard greens to keep him healthy, and he became a big guy, as I call him.

The word of the Lord tells us to train up a child in the way he should go and that he shall not depart from that way. When I read the word of God, I began to snatch my child out of the hand of the enemy. In my home there was always prayer. God kept him covered even in the streets. My son has had his own apartment now for several years, which makes me very happy and proud.

Boys are protective of their mothers, and Rashan remains that way. My son's life has turned around; he has a permanent job working for a good company. His job is building machines to test medications for hospitals. This job makes him happy and fulfilled. He tried the construction field, but a lot of the jobs went to the old-timers rather than the newcomers. With the economy so bad, jobs became hard to find, so he decided to try another avenue. I can say this new road had paid off for him.

Also I can say that he has rededicated his life to God and joined a new church.

My son also has a daughter named Myaira, whom he loves and takes shopping in the city every other weekend. This is their day out together, and she loves being her daddy's little girl, saying, "That's my daddy!" She makes that claim personal, as I used to do. On the way back to Jersey, they'll stop for lunch before catching the train.

My son has always been a blessing to me from the day he was born, and I thank God every day for giving me a son. There are times in our lives when we ask for certain things, but God knows what we need, and my son is my angel. He has been my main purpose for living and praying to God for strength to raise him by myself.

However, there was a time when my son started hanging out in the wrong places and getting into trouble. I continued talking to him and praying for him. Sometimes God would alert me that he was where he shouldn't be. I would get in my car, find him, and pick him up. There were many days when I picked him up—he didn't like it. In school he played on the football team, and I was proud of him. I expected him to play professionally and fly me all over the world. He was a natural; not going to practice was his downfall. His coach said he was good but skipped too many practices. I dropped him off at school, but he would leave early. The day I was told he couldn't play made me so mad because of his wasted talent.

He was trying to be one of the boys in the 'hood and wanted to fit in. However, he was different. I told him, "Everyone is different! Be yourself and accept who you are because it's important to like who you are." All around the clock, I worried about my son in the streets, though I couldn't watch him twenty-four hours a day. I had a friend who would call me when she spotted him in her complex so that I could come to pick him up. The moment my car reached the complex, people would say, "Here comes your mother." Sometimes he would hide, or others would hide him before I could get to him. If I could get to him before he saw me, it was all over; into the car and back home he would go.

On our way home, my son would say, "You are so embarrassing!"

I would then tell him, "Too bad! Get used to it! You're my son, and you're going to respect my name. It's important to me."

It finally got so bad he was caught, and I had to pick him up. That was a nightmare. I had not expected this kind of behavior from him. When it was time for court, I promised myself that if he was sentenced, I would not cry. When the judge said that he would serve time, however, even though it was his first time, I broke down and began to weep. I could not control my response.

I said, "Why didn't you listen? You didn't have to be out there! You had everything, and there was nothing you ever lacked. Why?" He just looked at me. Then we hugged, and I walked away.

The hand of God helped me through this crisis. That court date was a sad day in my life. The judge said, "I couldn't see the forest for the trees," which didn't feel good at all. After court I drove home, sad and wondering what I was going to do. I had not expected this to happen, not to my son. I had taught him better than that and raised him in a religious home with moral beliefs. With him gone, I felt as if somebody had died. In the morning I had to work, and my friends noticed the change in me and asked what was wrong. I began to tell them, and they encouraged me. Weekends were hard. It was then that I made my rounds. While driving, I would begin to cry and have to turn around and go home.

Not having my child with me was a hard pill to swallow. I began to blame myself and wonder what I might have done wrong. I fell into the routines that become very familiar to caring people who have loved ones in jail. While he was in jail, I would visit him. I took him care packages and clothes. Being able to see him was good, but I hated to leave him there. He was still in school at the time, and the school made arrangements to have him tutored to graduate high school. I thank God for those arrangements. It was important for him to finish high school. I believed very strongly in the necessity of finishing high school. He worked very hard to make sure all his subjects were completed and studied for his tests. The day he graduated, I was able to pick him up and bring him to the graduation with my family. This was a proud moment for all of us. The sad aspect was that he had to go back to the facility after the weekend was over. Once he finished doing his time, he came back home to stay with me. Our lives went well for a while, though I would later learn that my son was up to his old tricks.

Rashan's involvement with crime was a merry-go-round, a circular pattern repeated for at least ten years. I wondered when he would get enough of this life. The hand of God kept me functional during these rough years. Finally there came the last time he went away. By this point I didn't visit a lot, and he got mad. I didn't care because crime was a choice he had made. He had made his own bed and would now have to lie in it. I was at the point where I had to take care of myself or my whole head would be gray from worrying about my son. One day I looked in the mirror and saw my hair turning gray, a wake-up call to get myself together.

As I had done before in the wake of a crisis, I considered moving out of town and starting all over again. Where would I go? There was no plan; I just wanted to escape the hard ache. I had to lead devotions at church on the same day my son was locked up. I was asking myself how I was going to make my way through that day.

I parked my car at a hotel to collect my thoughts and pray for God's guidance and directions, which would help me through these years. There was a job that I was required to do at the church that day; I had to get myself together. I did win the victory on that night. I led devotions and expounded on all the speakers that night, and no one ever knew what had happened to me that day. God had been so good to me, and the power of prayer helped me through my challenges. I don't know how I would have endured my situation if I had not had God in my life and believed in the Creator. It's not easy to have an incarcerated adult child. Nor is it easy to figure out what to do when you have that burden *and* you're the sole breadwinner of the household. During such times, a person needs God to give her some extra strength to survive life on earth. When my son was on the right track as a kid, we would go to Disney World and to Florida in the summer. We would visit relatives; one year we went to Kansas City, Missouri, to a convention and to Chattanooga, Tennessee, for a family reunion. This family reunion was for my mother's side of the family. I would rent a two-room suite for us to stay in during the reunion.

Chapter 14
Tracing My Roots

Family ties, the connections of blood and kinship, have always been very important to me. I found out that my mother had a cousin living in Somerset, New Jersey, and attending one of the local churches. My mother was scheduled to go back with this cousin to North Carolina. This circumstance encouraged me, with God's guidance, to trace my roots and take a trip to North Carolina. I visited the city hall to look in the record books and found a sister about whom I had not known. I visited North Carolina for two weeks with my son, two godchildren, and a friend to help me drive. We stayed at the Cricket Inn, which was nice and brand-new.

I found that I had several cousins in this town also. My mother had a stepsister whom I met while visiting. I found my sister's father, who wouldn't tell me much about her, but I persisted and finally got a chance to meet her. She finally decided to see me, and I was happy to meet her. She wasn't happy about being given away at birth. I tried to explain to her, but she was hurt, and there was no turning back. We talked for a while. I got a chance to meet her son and daughter. Meeting and seeing me let them know they had some other relatives.

During these encounters, I had to do most of the talking. My friend sat by to help me. When I left my relatives, that closed a chapter in my life. During my stay in Greenville, North Carolina, I met a priest who taught me how to trace my roots. He gave me helpful suggestions concerning the information I needed to complete my journey.

After my husband died, I went to meet my mother, whom I hadn't seen since I was nine or ten years old. I took a plane to Kansas City, Missouri. Once I arrived, I called to let her know I was going to visit her soon. I collected my luggage and hopped onto the shuttle to the hotel to drop off my bags. I unpacked my clothes and called for a taxi. I remember that I was wearing a light blue slack set with a matching blue flowered blouse and a fashionable hairdo.

When I arrived at her building, one of the tenants let me into the hall. God's directions helped me too. I made my way to her apartment and knocked on her door; she opened the door and just stood there with her mouth open, not able to say a word.

Finally she said, "You look beautiful, and you've lightened up since the last time I saw you." When she had seen me the last time, I had been darker.

Mom welcomed me into her apartment with dinner. The table was set. I sat at the table with my brother, whom I was seeing for the very first time. My mom had had him after moving to Kansas City. She also had a male friend present for dinner, which was very nice. Her friend ate with us that day. During dinner we talked about my life and all the changes that had taken place in my life and in my mom's life in Kansas City. While I was there, we caught up. When night came, I went back to the hotel. She had invited me to stay with her, but I decided not. I told her that I had already paid for the room. To be honest, I hadn't seen my mother in such a long time that I wanted to get reacquainted with her first. I went back to the hotel until the next day, and then we got together to tour Kansas City. One night we went to see a movie. I was only there for a few days, and during this time, we tried to do as much as we could.

When it was time for me to go back home to New Jersey, she hated to see me leave. When I returned home, I kept in touch with her, writing letters and sending money for her and my brother to come visit me and the family. This was a surprise to her; they came around July 1974 and stayed with me. Sometimes my sister, who enjoyed my brother, would take him everywhere. My mother stayed with me because no one seemed to have room for her. I put her in my bed. She enjoyed staying with me because I took her everywhere I went—church, parties, the park, and shopping. I never left her behind, and we had a good time together. While at my apartment, my mother cooked for us, ironed my clothes, and mopped the floor. She tried to make up for lost time. I told her that wasn't possible and that we could only start with the present.

Chapter 15
My Mother Returns

God's hand allowed me to forgive my mom and let her get involved in my life again. I continued to live in my own apartment with my son, who was my heart and joy. My mother would travel with me wherever I went. However, after visiting in 1974, she went back to Kansas City for several years. After that time, she faced some changes. These changes made it necessary for her to be closer to her children in New Jersey. She left Kansas City and my brother, who was twenty-one at the time.

She moved back to New Brunswick and stayed with me again for a while. She felt I was her security blanket and did not want to stay with anyone else. One day it dawned on me that I felt smothered by this arrangement, and I told my mom, "You need to learn more about your other daughters." One of my younger sisters asked if Mom could stay with her, and she did stay with that sister. I would come by to check on Mom because she felt safe with me. When conversations with my other sisters got heated, I would always speak up for her.

My sister's place, however, wasn't Mom's last home. While at my sister's house, we filled out an application for Mom to get her own apartment. Later my mother moved into her own place, which she loved and adored. My mother got herself established by joining a local church in the community. She became a steward on the stewards' board and got involved in her residential complex. She did her own shopping, washing, cooking, and cleaning and took care of her own business. She was a very independent person; I believe I got my independence from her, though I also got it from my father, who started washing trucks at the age of seventeen. He later drove eighteen-wheelers from state to state for forty-one years, then drove locally until he retired. Life teaches us many lessons, and sometimes the best ones come from our parents' examples.

I learned from Mom by watching her and sometimes taking her advice. I respected her opinions, and her advice saved me a lot of heartaches over the years. Life can be a roller-coaster ride, but we have to keep moving through the rushing motion, knowing that God is there to bring us out safe. Some defeats come because of our own pain and circumstances, and we can't help anyone else out, but God can still use us even in our wounded hours. When I was in distress, I used to think that I could not help others, but God put people in my path for me to help, as with my mother.

Chapter 16
A Calling on My Life

After graduating from high school, I found out that I enjoyed typing and was good at it. My talent paid my bills. It also gave me the chance to carry out my calling from God in 1978.

Whenever I wasn't working, I would help people out by taking them to their doctors or to stores and just by talking to those people. I found that my presence meant a great deal to them. While I received widows' benefits, there was only a certain amount of money I could make. I spent my spare time helping those in need. For instance, my friend's godmother needed someone to take her to New York to the eye doctor, so he asked if I could take her. She and I would travel there by bus twice a month, and she enjoyed the trips. I called her Mrs. Wisdom because she was a wise woman, and everyone liked her.

In 1977 I traveled to Haiti. After returning from Haiti, I had a vision of myself in the hospitals, praying for the sick. In 1978 I head a trumpet blowing and saw a cloud over my head.

I had gone to Haiti during the summer with a girls' club. We visited Port-au-Prince and traveled into the mountains to take material to a new church. I remember many details of my time in Haiti. The mountain road seemed to go around and around. I met a minister during my time at that new church. The minister there asked if I would like to be a missionary, and I responded by saying that I didn't know if I had to come that far to Haiti. Later we visitors were given bananas and spring water. We also visited the minister's house before traveling back down the mountain. I enjoyed having chicken with black beans and rice for lunch. I loved Haiti. It's a beautiful country with lots of stars and beautiful beaches with clear water. The people were very nice to me every day. The people talked with me and said they could see my aura. My aura attracted them to me.

Back in the United States, I continued to work. My job consisted of entering doctors' orders, printing them out, separating each order, and matching orders to names. I had to put a copy into each nurse's box. My supervisor, who wanted to give me more responsibility without feeling threatened by me, saw how efficient I was. She decided to teach me how to key in time sheets, a task later assigned to me permanently. Time sheet entry was very easy.

Her timing was good because something happened to her husband while on vacation. She had to go out of state to see about him and left me to run work operations. I had never done transmissions before, but because she had to leave so soon, within an hour she had taught me how to transmit the material. There were three steps in this process. She went over the whole process so fast that she failed to break it down into steps for me. Overwhelmed, I asked a coworker for help. The coworker told me to go back to my supervisor and ask her to break the process down. The very next day, I asked her to explain it step by step. When she did so, the task became clearer to me, and I was able to prepare transmissions for that month. The transmissions consisted of all the work that had been entered into the computer. The process included a backup of all the work for the whole company. On the next day, I had to transmit everything over to another company to process our bills. This company would send the bills back to us with a check for services completed during the month.

When my supervisor returned, she learned about the good job I had done and was very happy. She said I could keep the position as a transmitter. Time went by, and the company grew. Its growth increased my workload, making it impossible to keep up with all the time sheets and forms. I had to inform my supervisor about the overload and have some tasks shifted from me to continue efficiently in my work. I liked time sheets most because they were easy and not as complicated as the forms. The forms were my babies, as my supervisor called them, and I was good at inputting them. She left me entering the doctors' orders and gave the time sheets to someone else to key into the computer.

In my work and in my faith, I have always taken my opportunities to expand my knowledge. The Spirit of God led me to continue my education. During the week, on Mondays after work, I attended Bible school in Newark. I received my bachelor's degree in theology and completed my thesis on the book of Revelation. This was hard to do because of the writing class I had to take at the same time. In the Bible school, everyone had to expound on the Word of God. My hermeneutics class gave me great practice for the future, and at times I was called to speak during chapel. When I finished school in Newark, I went on to Langhorne, Pennsylvania, to pursue a degree in counseling. I felt a need to learn more about the inner lives of people because of all the hurt I had experienced. I had attended many churches for more than seventeen years and still wanted to find a way of dealing with the pain. This class helped me realize that I was not alone in my pain. There were sixty other students beside me who had been hurt in different churches. When I applied to the college, there was an interview with the dean of the college. Then all the deans went out of the room for a while. Some returned and sat with me while we waited patiently for an answer. They opened the door and said, "You're accepted." I was so happy to receive that news and went back in September to register. Believe it or not, amidst all my academic efforts, I still worked a full-time job.

I attended college on Tuesdays and Thursdays and an additional night for a lab. Each week I had much reading material for homework. This schedule lasted for two years, and I took some weekend classes to complete this course. When it was time to graduate, I went for my cap and gown fitting. One of the professors approached me, saying I could not graduate with my class. He said I needed to see the dean. I went to meet with the dean to find out the problem. I learned that the school I had attended prior to that one wasn't accredited. If I wanted to receive my master's degree, I had to work on a bachelor's degree from an accredited school. My degree would be held on file until then.

That night I drove home, hurt and praying, with many thoughts and much disappointment. I wondered what to do next and tried to come up with a plan of action. I knew God had not brought me that far to leave me stranded. I continued doing the Lord's work. I was a member of a church and continued in fellowship there. I worked on the altar during deliverance and gave speeches. I did outreach ministry, which involved going to homes, hospitals, prisons, and mental institutions. I passed out tracts and Bibles and tried to encourage men and women.

One day a friend told me about a university in Madison, New Jersey. I applied for a continuing education program there and was accepted. My first course was psychology. There were many young people in the class. The course dealt with parts of the brain and brain functions.

Our teacher was new in her position, and her method of teaching made testing very difficult. Whatever we had studied would not be on the test. Sometimes the test material was worded in such a way that I had no idea what was meant. I was happy when the course was over, and I hoped to take a subject that was more interesting. The course I found was sociology, which dealt with different issues. I fit into this class; we had many discussions on all topics of the present and the 1800s. The professor appreciated having me in the class. One day she said that it was "good to have a mature adult in the class" because the students were young and there was not enough feedback in class. When the course was over, I took a break from college because this was going to be a long progression toward my destination. I continued to work every day from 8:30 AM to 4:40 PM. I was invited to register at a hospital to receive a certificate in pastoral care, so I applied. I was accepted with a partial scholarship and was responsible for only five hundred dollars. God's hand was in my decision to take the course, get a scholarship, and complete it.

The course in pastoral care would last ten months and involve working a set number of hours every day. I also had to work in different units in the hospital. My day started after work and extended from 5:00–5:30 p.m. until 9:00 p.m. or later, according to need. The departments I chose were the MCI and ICU and the rehabilitation and maternity wards. On the weekends I took care of the emergency room. I was on call every night while at the hospital, carrying a beeper at all times. During the week I had to produce a verbatim statement. This document was a word-for-word record of what I had said to a patient and the response. Once a week my group would meet to discuss the verbatim statements and give feedback.

There was also an impression report due. My instructor wanted to know how my week went, so she would meet with me to go over that report and ask questions. I can say this was a positive course that enhanced my abilities. I was enlightened; this class opened new doors for me. It gave me great opportunities to help people. I graduated with a certificate in pastoral care. After taking the course, I found out that if a person was an ordained minister, the class was not necessary to become a chaplain.

I'm glad about the time I spent helping to brighten patients' days in the hospital. We all have a story to tell and need a listening ear to hear what we have to say.

I was still trying to get my bachelor's degree and waiting for a door to open for me. Well, while I was working in home care, one day I got a call from Philadelphia Biblical University. They told me about a new program, Advance in Leadership, and asked if I would be interested in taking this course. I said, "Sure. Send me some information." God's hand was in the knowledge of this newly developed program.

I filled out the application and was accepted into the program. I started school in September, attending classes every Thursday night after work. My location was good; I could take all the back roads, which made my trip shorter and less traffic-ridden. I learned to enjoy the academic work I did on the way to my goals. My workload was a hard course in Biblical studies and had an emphasis on articulating one's points. With the help of God, I completed my stidies. During the graduation dinner after the rehearsal, I reflected on God's goodness.

The day of my graduation was a proud one for me. I invited my friends and family to come and celebrate with me. The people present were my mom, my son, and my friend. My mom was so proud of me and was of one my best supporters. She was happy about all my accomplishments and remained eager to travel with me, whatever the distance. At my graduation, I was excited as we waited in the hallway to be called. When I entered the gym and saw all those people, I said "Wow!" and continued to my seat. When my name was called, "Rebecca E. McMillan," I was so proud! I know that my expression showed my pleasure at reaching my goal!

All my life I've had to take care of myself. As I have mentioned, I worked to buy clothes at a young age. In the midst of all my striving, it had never entered my mind that I might be college material. College became a personal consideration when I went to a local church for Bible study. I received certificates in Biblical studies and evangelism. My girlfriend, whom I called Mrs. Administrator, suggested, "Why don't you come with me and Ms. J to Newark's Bible College? They will give you credit for all those certificates, and you can get a degree."

I thank God for Mrs. Administrator and Mrs. Hospitality, who helped pave the way for me. She helped type my papers and my thesis in Newark. We went to the Bible school for two years; my friend was very helpful and knowledgeable.

After a vivid dream, it was my goal to get my degree in counseling. In my dream, I was in a room with a desk. The room had three tiers, somewhat like a theater. When I arrived at the College of Philadelphia Biblical University, I found that the classroom was like the room I saw in my dream. This is how I knew it was God's plan for me to be there. I told the dean about my dream to make events unfold effectively for me. I had to have a plan of action and be on point when the time came to speak. I had to articulate my needs so they could and would be met.

After graduation I continued to work in home care for sixteen years. I was vested in the 401K after five years, an important way to build a nest for myself.

A change eventually came to my workplace after September 11, 2001. In 2006 my hours were reduced to twenty-two per week with no benefits. Then I learned that my job was cut as of October 2006.

My supervisor brought me into the CEO'S office and said, "We have something to tell you."

I asked, "What?" Then they hit me with the news that my position was no longer available. This was because the nurses had received laptops and were inputting their own orders. I looked at them and said, "Thank you." I could see the handwriting on the wall. However, I should note that I was able to finish college while working at that job and that it put me closer to Pennsylvania.

On my way out of the office, the supervisor and the CEO hugged me, and I walked back to my desk. One of my coworkers saw me and asked, "Are you all right?" I said, "Yes, God is still good and has a plan for my life. I'll be all right. This will give me time to look for something else."

My reasons for working were earning enough to pay my bills and helping people. It wasn't enough for me just to pay my bills, so I continued to work and do ministry on the side. After work I was called to help those in need, and my heart's desire was to help battered woman. One of the papers I wrote for college addressed this desire. After I completed a course on sexual addiction, I wrote a paper on battered women. My paper reflected my hunger to help those who have been used, rejected, and abused.

In those and my other endeavors, God had been good to me and guided me all the way. God will show us the directions in which we are to go. I could picture what I wanted to do and the road I wanted to travel.

Now I am standing, strong as the hand of God, which has guided me along all the paths of my life! I am in a career school and training as a computer specialist. I have learned several programs—PowerPoint, Excel, Mail Merge, and QuickBooks. This expertise will make me more marketable in the future. I am still in ministry and looking forward to the day when I will have my own church. My church will be a place where people can come to be healed and encouraged.

Epilogue

Reverend Dr. Charlie H. Brown, Jr.

I would like to encourage each of us to get a copy of Reverend Rebecca McMillan's book. She is indeed a Christian soldier of God's followers. Years ago, when I was in Saint Peter's Hospital for my heart, she came into my room with her Bible and other tools needed for a sacred moment with me. Her reading of the Scriptures and her words of prayer really moved me inside my soul. Her visit was so effective that I asked the Lord, "Does she really have to leave so soon?" After her visit at my bedside, I watched her make her way back through those doors, going back to church or to another room. She would stop by and pray for different people on the floor who expressed a need.

I am honored to say a few words for her book. I would like to congratulate her on this great effort and encourage her to continue her thoughts.

Reverend Dr. Charlie H. Brown, Jr. is a retired military man with over forty years of service and the senior pastor of the First Baptist Church of Lincoln Gardens in Somerset, New Jersey.

Dedication

Many of my loved ones deserve a mention in the dedication of my book.

I dedicate my book to my one and only son, Rashan McMillan, whom I raised from the age of six months by myself after the death of his father. Rashan was my protector, even at an early age. He still is.

I dedicate my book to my mother, Teddy Marie Bradford, who died March 28, 2005. Still young in the spirit, she died at the age of eighty. My best supporter, she loved me very much and traveled with me whenever I had to go out to preach.

I dedicate my book to the one who helped raise me when my mother wasn't around for a while, Mrs. Rosetta Robertson. She took care of me and always said that she saw me walking in white in the hospitals because of my desire to help others.

I dedicate my book to Ma Dear, who was instrumental in my life when I came to stay with my father at the age of seventeen. She got me more involved with fashion. She entered me in fashion shows and encouraged me to enter a beauty contest, which I won, becoming Ms. Elks. She was a very strong woman who didn't mind taking care of those who were in distress and needed a helping hand. She always gave her support as a foster parent.

I dedicate my book to Leslie Jackson-Brown, my friend who edited my book. She always helped me while I was in college. She is one with whom I have remained friends for over thirty years.

I dedicate my book to my friend Gwen Livingston, whom I have known since my childhood years.

I dedicate my book to Martha, who encouraged me to keep writing even after my job ended.

Rebecca E. McMillan

I dedicate my book to my siblings: my sisters Gloria, Carolyn, and Shirley and my brother Mo, who lives in Kansas City. God has been good to Marvin and has kept us connected and sharing our love.

Printed in the United States
By Bookmasters